The Peoples and Cultures of New York

James Bernard

New York

Published in 2015 by The Rosen Publishing Group, Inc.
29 East 21st Street, New York, NY 10010

Book Design: Chris Brand

Photo Credits: Cover Universal Images Group/Getty Images; p. 5 DircinhaSW/Moment/Getty Images; p. 7 © Archivo Incongrafico, S.A./Corbis; p. 9 Art Resource, NY; p. 11 Library of Congress Prints and Photographs Division, Washington, DC; p. 13 Thomas Reese/Moment/Getty Images; p. 15 © Kevin Fleming/Corbis; p. 15 (inset) © Michael Tamborrino/FPG International; p. 17 Hulton Archive/Stringer/Getty Images; p. 19 Slaven Vlasic/Stringer/Getty Images Entertainment/Getty Images; p. 21 (top row, bottom left) MPI/Stringer/Archive Photos/Getty Images; p. 21 (bottom right) Gilles Petard/Redfems/Getty Images.

Library of Congress Cataloging-in-Publication Data

Bernard, James.
The peoples and cultures of New York / by James Bernard.
p. cm. — (Spotlight on New York)
Includes index.
ISBN 978-1-4777-7339-0 (pbk.)
ISBN 978-1-4777-7290-4 (6-pack)
ISBN 978-1-4777-7322-2 (library binding)
1. Immigrants—New York (State)—New York—Juvenile literature. 2. Minorities—New York (State)—New York—Juvenile literature. 3. New York (N.Y.)—Emigration and immigration—Juvenile literature. I. Bernard, James. II. Title.
F128.9.A1 B47 2015
305.8009747—d23

Manufactured in the United States of America

CPSIA Compliance Information: Batch #WS15RC: For further information contact Rosen Publishing, New York, New York at 1-800-237-9932.

Contents

What Is Culture?

The United States is often said to be one **nation** with many cultures. What exactly does that mean? In order to answer that question, we first need to know what culture is. Culture is a way of life shared by members of a specific population. Culture includes beliefs, attitudes, customs, and material creations such as art.

Cultures are not **static**. They change over time for many different reasons. For example, computers and the Internet have changed the way many of us communicate, seek information, shop, and pay our bills. This change occurred within the culture of the United States through the introduction of new technology.

Another way that culture can change is through the introduction of elements from an outside culture. The **multicultural** identity of the United States was shaped by the different cultural and ethnic groups that have come to call this country home.

If you want to write to a friend or family member, you can use the Internet to send them an e-mail or an instant message. Fifty years ago, you would have had to write them a letter and have it delivered by the post office. The Internet changed the way we communicate. It changed our culture.

New York:
A Multicultural Beginning

New York State is a good example of what it means to be a multicultural **society**. Before the first Europeans arrived, the land that would become New York State was home to different groups of Native Americans, each with their own beliefs, customs, and traditions. Thousands of Native Americans live in New York today. The influence of Native American cultures can be seen today in the names of places like Niagara Falls, Poughkeepsie, Manhattan, and Montauk.

New Netherland, the Dutch colony that was renamed New York by the English, was settled by different ethnic and cultural groups. In addition to the Dutch, New Netherland attracted Irish, Scandinavian, and French settlers. Other groups included French-speaking **Walloons**, Germans from the western German states, and Africans who had been brought to the colony as **slaves**.

Each group that came to New Netherland brought its beliefs, traditions, and customs. In addition to the different cultural groups living within New Netherland, there was an influence of French culture coming from New France to the north and English culture to the east. People from these diverse cultures helped shape New York State.

Many early immigrants came to New York from Europe. This map, made about 1570, shows Europe at the time when Europeans first began emigrating to America.

Why Did Immigrants Come to New York?

When we talk about immigration to New York State, we often focus on the waves of mass immigration that occurred in the nineteenth century, first from northern and western Europe and later from southern and eastern Europe. There is no single reason why these groups came to the state. Many different factors contributed to immigration.

During the nineteenth century, there was political unrest and **poverty** in many parts of the world. Modern countries like Germany and Italy did not exist. Instead, there were numerous independent Italian and German states. Fighting between these states made them difficult places to live. Crop failures in Ireland and the German states also forced people to look for other places to live.

New York State had a lot to offer immigrants. The **Industrial Revolution** was changing the state. Inventors and engineers from Europe brought **innovations** from Europe to America. Laborers were needed to work in factories and other businesses that were being built in cities like Buffalo, Rochester, and New York City. Labor was also needed for large construction jobs, such as building **canals** and railroads. These canals and railroads also opened up land for development, which attracted immigrants from the overcrowded parts of Europe.

As the United States grew, workers were needed for large construction projects, like building canals and laying track for the railroads. Immigrants, like these Irish immigrants, provided much-needed labor.

The Difficulties Faced by Immigrants

Life was not easy for many new immigrants. Some left their families and possessions behind and arrived in this country with little more than the clothes on their back. Many immigrants faced hostility from Americans who believed that native-born Americans were superior to the new arrivals. Immigrants were often used as **scapegoats** during bad economic times. They were sometimes blamed for taking jobs away from citizens who had lived here longer. Some immigrants were blamed for the rise in crime, as well.

When immigrants came to the United States, they brought their own customs and beliefs with them. Many of these customs appeared strange to native-born Americans. This led to misunderstandings and **prejudice**.

The language barrier was the biggest **obstacle** that new immigrants faced. It was difficult to find a job because employers did not want to hire people who didn't speak English. The language barrier also made it easy for dishonest people to take advantage of new immigrants.

In the mid-1850s, a political party known as the Know Nothings spoke out against immigration, especially Irish Catholics. This group often resorted to violence against immigrants. The Know Nothing Party began as secret societies. When asked about membership, the leaders would say, "I know nothing."

UNCLE SAM'S YOUNGEST SON

CITIZEN

KNOW NOTHING.

11

Ethnic Enclaves and Immigrant Societies

Because of the difficulties they faced, immigrants formed support systems in their new home. Immigrants from the same part of the world often settled in the same neighborhood. Sometimes, these neighborhoods would be home to immigrants from the same town or village.

Living with other immigrants provided a sense of security for new arrivals. It also allowed the immigrants to keep the language and customs of their homeland alive. Many large cities still have **enclaves**—neighborhoods with names like Koreatown or Little Italy. Prejudice and hostility from native-born Americans often **compelled** ethnic groups to remain in these enclaves.

Another means of support for new immigrants came in the form of immigrant societies, sometimes called hometown or **benefit** societies. These groups were established by immigrants from the same region to deal with the social, economic, and cultural problems that new immigrants faced.

Many neighborhoods, like Manhattan's Little Italy, began as ethnic enclaves where immigrants from the same part of the world could find a sense of community and security. Today, tourists and locals visit Little Italy to visit the neighborhood's Italian stores and restaurants.

Immigrants Help New York State Grow

As a center of **commerce**, New York City was the destination for ships from around the world, making it the point of entry for many immigrants. While some immigrants spread throughout the country, many remained in New York State. These new arrivals played an important role in the growth of New York State throughout the nineteenth and twentieth centuries.

After the **American Revolution**, New York State saw a period of rapid growth. This growth provided opportunities for those willing to take advantage of them. Farmland attracted **migrants** from New England, as well as immigrants from southern Germany. The transportation networks that helped open up New York State were built, in part, by immigrant labor. As industrial cities developed in central and western New York, immigrants filled many of the jobs in factories. Cities like Albany, Buffalo, Syracuse, and Rochester grew rapidly thanks to the waves of immigrants that came to the state.

This photograph shows Ellis Island as it looks today. The Statue of Liberty, shown in the small photograph, can be seen from Ellis Island. Since 1886, the statue has been a symbol of a new life for many immigrants. Emma Lazarus, a Jewish woman from New York, wrote a famous poem welcoming immigrants to America that appears on the base of the statue.

Irish and German Immigrants

Immigration from Ireland and the German states occurred during New York's colonial period. However, the middle of the nineteenth century saw large waves of immigrants coming from these areas. Poor harvests in Ireland and central Europe led to food shortages and a flood of rural poor into Europe's urban areas. European cities became overcrowded and jobs were hard to find, so people looked to the United States for new opportunities.

Although some Irish immigrants became farmers, most worked in construction jobs across New York State. Irish laborers worked on canals and railroads. Irish communities developed in the cities along the Erie Canal, as well as in the New York City area. Irish immigrants also contributed to New York State's literature, music, and theater.

Many German immigrants were artists, craftsmen, and tradesmen, and they brought these skills with them when they came to New York State. German immigrants became **prominent** in the garment industry, retail, and banking. Scientists and inventors from Germany helped New York's industrialization. German craftsmen made New York State a leader in the production of musical instruments, like the famous Steinway pianos built by Manhattan's Steinway & Sons.

The art, literature, and music of the United States benefited from the contributions made by immigrants and the children of immigrants. The son of an Irish immigrant father and an Irish American mother, Eugene O'Neill was an award-winning playwright.

Italian and Eastern European Immigrants

Small groups of Italian immigrants could be found working as musicians, artists, and shopkeepers in Rochester and Utica since the 1850s. However, the largest wave of Italian immigrants did not arrive in New York State until after the **American Civil War**. Most were men from central and southern Italian regions, who came to work construction jobs in the Hudson River valley, Rochester, Utica, and Albany. Like previous waves of immigrants, Italian immigrants were also drawn to the growing **manufacturing** cities that grew along the Erie Canal.

At the same time that Italian immigrants were arriving in large numbers, there was also a rise in immigration from eastern Europe and Russia. Many of these immigrants were Ashkenazi Jews who were escaping **pogroms** in the Russian Empire, as well as the economic pressures that were becoming common across Europe at the time. Jewish immigrants settled in cities like Buffalo, Rochester, and New York City, where they worked as shopkeepers, tailors, clothing dealers, carpenters, and watchmakers. Yiddish theater, a mix of musical comedy, drama, and **satire**, became a popular attraction for both Jewish and non-Jewish Americans.

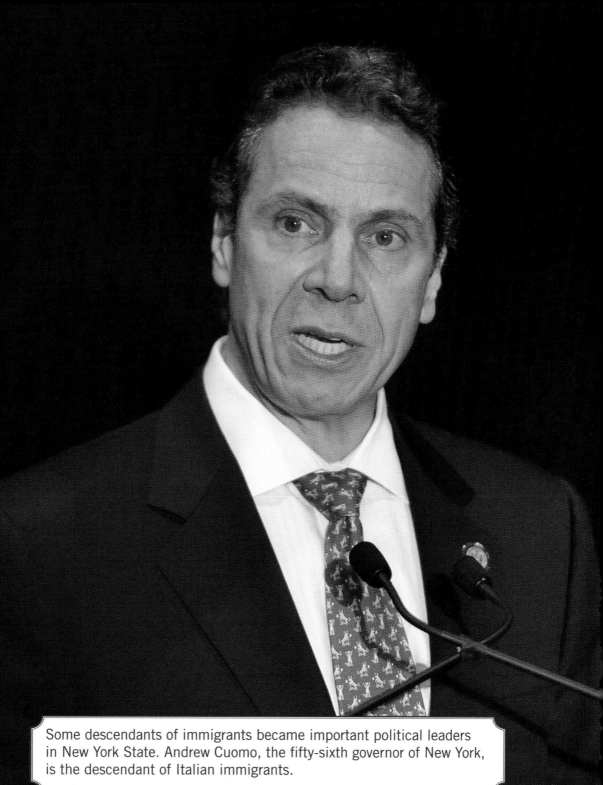

Some descendants of immigrants became important political leaders in New York State. Andrew Cuomo, the fifty-sixth governor of New York, is the descendant of Italian immigrants.

The Great Migration and the Harlem Renaissance

The first Africans were brought to New Netherland as slaves around 1626. While some slaves gained their freedom over time, most remained enslaved until 1827, when a law freed all enslaved New Yorkers. In the first half of the nineteenth century, New York State became a center of the **abolitionist** movement to end slavery nationwide. Buffalo, Rochester, and Syracuse were all stops on the Underground Railroad that helped southern slaves escape to freedom.

During the early twentieth century, a large number of southern African Americans began to migrate north. Despite slavery ending after the Civil War, the South was still a difficult and **oppressive** place for African Americans. They were drawn to the employment opportunities in New York's industrial cities and farms. African Americans were often met with **racism** and hostility by white northerners.

Many African Americans lived in Manhattan's Harlem, which became a center for their culture. During the 1920s, the works of African American musicians, writers, dancers, and artists became known around the world. This period of artistic creativity became known as the Harlem Renaissance. Themes addressed by artists of the Harlem Renaissance included the African American quest for racial identity and political and social equality.

Frederick Douglass

Langston Hughes

Sojourner Truth

Billie Holiday

New York State was home to abolitionists like Frederick Douglass and Sojourner Truth. They played important roles in the movement to end slavery in the United States. During the early twentieth century, New York City's Harlem was home to artists, musicians, and writers like Langston Hughes and Billie Holiday.

Immigration in the Twentieth and Twenty-First Centuries

The greatest impact on immigration in the twentieth century came from the United States government. The Immigration Restriction Act of 1921 was the first federal law to limit immigration from European countries. Earlier laws, like the Chinese Exclusion Act, limited immigration from non-European countries, but this law limited immigration from southern and eastern Europe. The Immigration Restriction Act was revised in 1924 to further **restrict** immigration by creating quotas that favored northern Europeans.

Forty years later, the Immigration Act of 1965 removed all restrictions based on nationality. This law led to New York State seeing a wave of immigrants from non-European countries. Immigrants from the Dominican Republic, China, Jamaica, Guyana, Haiti, India, Colombia, and Ecuador added to the racial and ethnic diversity of cities like Rochester, Utica, Buffalo, Syracuse, Albany, and New York City. As with past waves of immigrants, these new arrivals came to the United States to escape political unrest or economic **hardships** back home. And, like the immigrants who came before them, they all contribute to the multicultural identity of New York State.

Glossary

abolitionist: A person who supports the end of slavery.

American Civil War: The war that was fought between the Northern states of the Union and the Southern states of the Confederacy between 1861 and 1865.

American Revolution: The war that the American colonists fought from 1775 to 1783 to win independence from England.

benefit: Something that improves, promotes, or assists.

canals: Man-made waterways.

commerce: Business or trade.

compelled: Caused to occur by overwhelming pressure.

enclaves: Small areas or groups enclosed or isolated within larger ones.

hardships: Difficulties.

Industrial Revolution: The period in history when the means of production shifted from hand tools to power-driven machines.

innovations: New ideas, devices, or ways of doing something.

manufacturing: Producing goods.

migrants: People who move from one country, region, or place to another.

multicultural: Representing several different cultures.

nation: A large area of land that is controlled by its own government.

obstacle: A person or thing that makes it difficult to do something.

oppressive: Very cruel, unpleasant, or uncomfortable.

pogroms: Slaughters of a religious or ethnic group, particularly Jews, organized and carried out by a government.

poverty: The state of having little or no money or material possessions.

prejudice: An unfavorable opinion formed without knowledge, thought, or reason.

prominent: Important or well-known.

racism: Hatred or intolerance of other races or ethnic groups based upon the belief that your race or ethnic group is superior.

restrict: To limit the amount of something.

satire: Humor that shows the weaknesses or bad qualities of a person, group, government, or society.

scapegoats: People or groups that are unfairly blamed.

slaves: People who are treated as property to be bought, sold, and forced to work.

society: The people thought of as living together in organized communities with shared laws, traditions, and values.

static: Showing little or no change.

Walloons: A French-speaking people who live in southern and southeastern Belgium.

Index

Primary Source List

Page 7. *Map of Europe.* Created by Abraham Ortelius, published in *Theatrum Orbis Terrarum.* 1570. Now kept at the Library of Congress Geography and Map Division, Washington, DC.

Page 9. *Photograph of Erie Canal.* ca. 1820.

Page 11. *Uncle Sam's Youngest Son, Citizen Know Nothing.* Created by Sarony & Co., published by Williams, Stevens, Williams & Co. Lithographic print. 1854. Now kept at the Library of Congress Prints and Photographs Division, Washington, DC.

Page 21 (top right). *Mr. Langston Hughes, Negro poet and playwright. Chicago, Illinois.* Created by Jack Delano. Photographic print. 1942. Now kept at the Library of Congress Prints and Photographic Prints, Washington, DC.

Page 21 (bottom left). *Sojourner Truth, three-quarter length portrait, standing, wearing spectacles, shawl, and peaked cap, right hand resting on cane.* Photographic print. 1864. Now kept at the Library of Congress Prints and Photographs Division, Washington, DC.

Websites

Due to the changing nature of Internet links, The Rosen Publishing Group, Inc. has developed an online list of websites related to the subjects of this book. This site is updated regularly. Please use this link to access the list: **http://www.rcbmlinks.com/nysh/pcny**